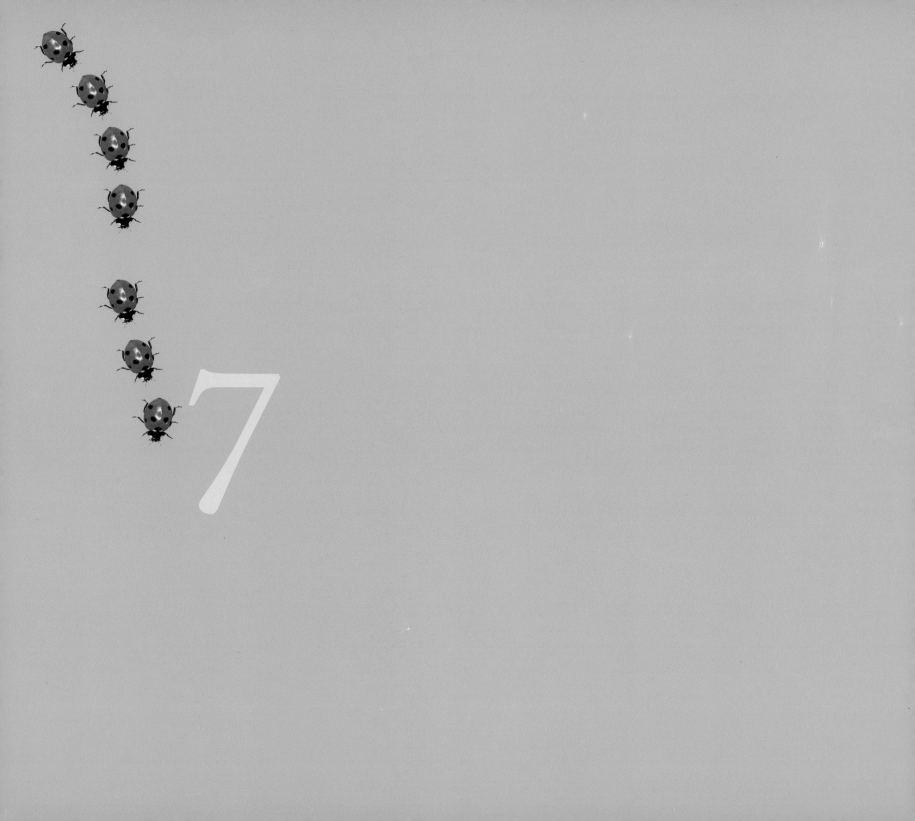

7

Numbers

1

PLAY BAC
PUBLISHING
More.Brain.Power

Nature is an excellent math teacher!

To learn to count from 1 to 12, all you have to do is look at nature!
A rabbit has 2 ears, clover has 4 leaves, a starfish has 5 arms, and insects have 6 legs.
For sums, it's just as simple.
In this book, penguins teach us how to add, ants how to subtract.
Counting cherries enables us to multiply, and cutting an orange helps us to understand the principle of division.
The world around us can help us to discover odd and even numbers, to rank objects from smallest to largest, to compare, to group, and to learn.

1 one

Does this tree stand alone?
Is this dog lonely?
Of course not!
Because 1 is the first in a long family of numbers!

2 two

Are you seeing double? On this page everything comes in twos! Two ears make a pair, the cherries are twins, and these pink flamingos are a couple!

3 three

One, two, three. . . GO!
Three ants carrying three leaves.
Three lion cubs feeling the breeze.

4 four

*Two in front, two behind,
All four legs get us there quickly!
Two in front, two behind,
All four legs are furry
and prickly!*

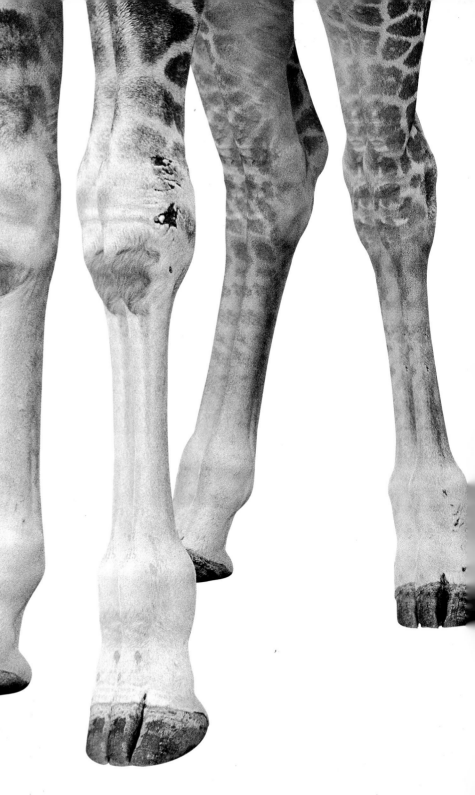

5 five

Five zebra brothers looking for another.

6 six

Six-legged beetle, searching for some food,
Six petals, six leaves, and six toadstools!

7 seven

How many carrots can you see?
There are seven, one for each day of the week!
Now isn't that practical?

8 eight

A circle above,
And a circle below.
One circle on top of the other
Makes a number you should know:
The figure 8!

9 nine

Out of these speckled eggs so fine
Will hatch lots of chicks . . . I'd say nine!

10 ten

A 1 and a 0. That's not a lot!
But put them together and see what you've got!

11 eleven

Two number 1s side by side,
Eleven starfish, nowhere to hide.

12 twelve

When a 1 and 2 get together, that makes twelve!
I don't have enough fingers, so I'll count bunnies instead!

Now you count!

How many yellow fish can you see?
Silver fish? Goldfish?
More than three?

Numbers
in sequence

1st 2nd 3rd 4th

1st

2nd

3rd

First is in front.
Second comes next.
Third follows slowly.
Fourth brings up the rear!

A lot   A little

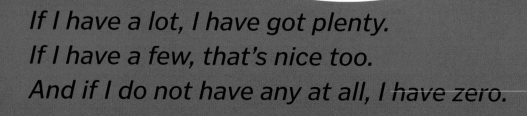

If I have a lot, I have got plenty.
If I have a few, that's nice too.
And if I do not have any at all, I have zero.

None at all

zero

Ten

You need ten pelicans to make a ten.

10

Hun[d]

Ten times ten equals a hundred.

red **100**

Thousands

Ten times a hundred birds, oh my!
Equals one thousand and that's no lie!

1000

From the smallest

A quail's egg is smaller than a hen's egg.
A hen's egg is smaller than an ostrich's egg.
From the smallest to the largest, that's increasing order.

o the largest

From the largest

to the smallest

The grapefruit is the largest,
the orange comes next,
before the clementine, which is much smaller.
From the largest to the smallest, that's decreasing order.

As many as

Three strawberries on the left,
Three strawberries on the right.
There are as many on the left as on the right.
So the two sides are *equal*!

More than

There are more bananas than pears,
Add them up, don't despair!
And everyone agrees,
there are fewer blueberries than pea

Less than

Even

Group the turtles two by two!
If they all have a friend,
There is an even number.
And with an even number,
You always get pairs!

2
4
6
8

Odd

1 3 5 7 9

But if one turtle is left alone
When all the others are in pairs,
One turtle has no partner and
There is an odd number of them.

Addition

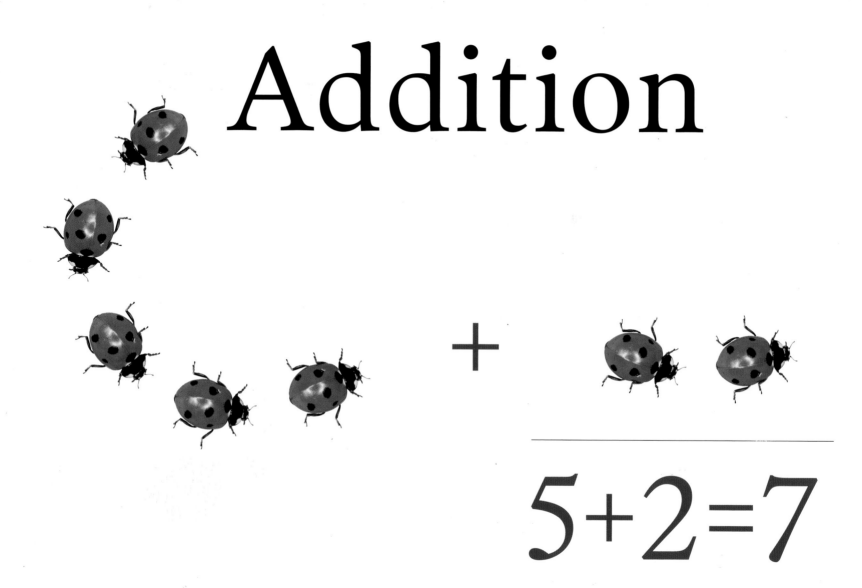

$$5+2=7$$

Who are these latecomers adding themselves
to the circle of ladybugs?
There were five, now there are seven!
That's the idea of addition.

Subtraction

Five ants are on their way home.
One leaves the others on their own.
There are only four of them now.
And you've done subtraction, wow!

5-1= 4

4-1= 3

Multiplication

*I picked two cherries, another two,
then two more.
I picked two cherries three times.
That's multiplication!
I picked six cherries in all, and now
I'm going to eat them!*

$$2 \times 3 = 6$$

$2 \times 2 = 4$

Division

Everyone is happy. They all have the same size portion!
Because division means sharing in equal parts.

$$1 \div 2 = \frac{1}{2}$$

If you divide an orange in two, you get two halves.
If you cut those halves in two, you get four quarters!

$$1 \div 4 = \frac{1}{4}$$

Now, you count!

Is there an odd number or an even number of yellow butterflies?
Are there more white butterflies than speckled butterflies?
And if the big blue butterfly flies away, how many blue ones are left?

Acknowledgments:

Play Bac Publishing wishes to thank all the teachers, mothers, and children who have helped develop the **eye like** series

SPECIAL THANKS to: Frédéric Michaud, Claire Despine, Anne Burrus, Beryl Motte, Munira Al-Khalili, Elizabeth Van Houten and Paula Manzanero

All the books in the Play Bac series have been tested by families and teachers and edited and proofread by professionals in the field.

Copyright © 2007 by Play Bac Publishing USA, Inc.

ISBN-13 : 978-1-60214-019-6

Play Bac Publishing USA, Inc.
225 Varick Street, New York, NY 10014-4381

Printed in Singapore by TWP

Distributed by
Black Dog & Leventhal Publishers, Inc.
151 West 19th Street, New York, NY 10011

First printing, September 2007

Photography credits:

Meaning of the letters:
h : top ; b : bottom ; d : right ; g : left ; c : center.

COLIBRI : LAVERGNE J.-Y. : 36g ; TABONI J. : 36d.

GETTY : ATKINSON P. : 25 ; BENELUX PRESS : 16 ; BRAUN F. & HERF A. : 18b ; CLAMER M. : 10 ; COELFEN E. : 49g ; DOLE J. : 21h ; DOYLE P. : 4 ; ELSDALE B. : 47 ; ELZENGA J. : 9 ; FLACH T. : 8 ; GORTON S. & RONCHI Z. : 23 ; GRAUBART A. : 14d ; HART V. & G.K. : 6g, 26&27 ; JONATHAN & ANGELA : 38 ; KANTOR J. : 51 ; KELLY J. : 30 ; KLOVE L. : 42d ; KRAHMER F. : front cover/d ; LEMENS F. : 7, 34 ; LILLIE P. : 37 ; LING B. : 44h, 45h ; MCINTYRE N. : 49d ; MONTROSE S. : 21b ; ROSENFELD M. : 17hd, 43hd ; RYNIO J. : 32 & 33 ; SHUMWAY G. : 18h ; SMITH R. : 11b and back cover ; TAYLOR K. : 44b & 45b ; TEUBNER CH. : 32g, 43bg ; VAN OS J. : 19, front cover/g ; VASAN G. : 31 ; WALKER J. : 5 ; WARWICK J. : 12 & 13 ; WASSERFALL R. : 41.

SUNSET : ALASKA STOCK : 22 ; CATTLIN N. : 26h ; DELFINO D. : 35 ; FLPA : 20 ; HOSKING D. : 34&35 ; LACZ G. : 11 ; MARGE : 15.

MARC SCHWARTZ : 17b, 39c, 52d, 52g & 53g, 53d, front cover/bd and spine.

OTHER PHOTOS : DR.

In the same series: